WEST VIRGINIA

in words and pictures

BY DENNIS B. FRADIN

ILLUSTRATIONS BY RICHARD WAHL

MAPS BY LEN W. MEENTS

Consultant:
Otis K. Rice
West Virginia Institute
of Technology

CHILDRENS PRESS ™

CHICAGO

To Bernard Brindel, a lifelong inspiration

Fall colors in the hills of West Virginia

Library of Congress Cataloging in Publication Data

Fradin, Dennis B
  West Virginia in words and pictures.

  SUMMARY: A history and description of the Mountain
State
  1. West Virginia—Juvenile literature. [1. West
Virginia] I. Wahl, Richard, 1939- II. Meents,
Len W. III. Title.
F241.3.F73   975.4   80-12133
ISBN 0-516-03949-0

Picture Acknowledgments:
GOVERNOR'S OFFICE OF ECONOMIC AND COMMUNITY
DEVELOPMENT: cover, 31 (right), 34, 36 (right), 37 (left), 41;
PHOTOGRAPHS BY GERALD S. RATLIFF, 2, 4, 5, 7, 15, 21, 24, 25, 26
27, 29 (left), 30, 31 (left), 32, 33, 39, 40; PHOTOGRAPH BY STEVE
PAYNE, 14; PHOTOGRAPH BY DAVID SIMPSON, 37 (right);
PHOTOGRAPHS BY TOM EVANS, 19, 23; PHOTOGRAPH BY DAVE
CRUISE, 36 (left)
UPPER OHIO VALLEY TRAVEL COUNCIL: 13, 28 (right), 29 (right)
HUNTINGTON CONVENTION & VISITORS BUREAU: 18
WEST VIRGINIA UNIVERSITY OFFICE OF PUBLICATIONS: 28 (left)
COVER PICTURE: A farm scene in Pendleton County

West Virginia

West Virginia is nicknamed the *Mountain State.* Mountains and hills cover most of the state. Farmers often have to grow their crops on hills. They joke about "falling off the sides" of their corn fields.

West Virginia is a lovely state. Rivers flow through the valleys. Hardwood forests cover the mountains. Towns nestle in the hills. There are many coal-mining towns. West Virginia is a leading coal-mining state.

West Virginia has much more. Where was the last battle of the Revolutionary War (rev • oh • LOO • shun • airy WORE) fought? Where was the first land battle of the Civil War? Where do scientists listen to radio waves from outer space? Where was General "Stonewall" Jackson born? As you will learn, the answer to these questions is the Mountain State — West Virginia.

3

About 300 million years ago the land was covered by swamps. Plants grew in the shallow water. The plants died. They formed a thick layer of plant material. Over millions of years this hardened into coal.

If you push the ends of a rug together, it will rise in the middle. In this way the Appalachian (app • ah • LAY • chen) Mountains were folded from the earth, about 200 million years ago.

The first people came to West Virginia at least 10,000 years ago. One early group of Indians is called the Mound Builders. They lived here about 3,000 years ago. They piled dirt into hills, called *mounds*. Some mounds— such as Grave Creek Mound—were used to bury the

Grave Creek Mound, Moundsville

4

Indian mounds, South Charleston

dead. Skeletons have been found inside. Other mounds were big forts. Farm tools prove that the Mound Builders grew crops. Spears prove that they hunted. Their pottery and jewelry have also been found.

The Mound Builders may have been related to the Indians who came later. Some of the tribes were the Shawnee (shaw • NEE), Delaware (DELL • ah • ware), and Susquehanna (suss • kwah • HAN • uh).

The Indians hunted bison, deer, and elk. They ate the meat. They used the skins to make clothes. Indians also fished in West Virginia rivers.

5

West Virginia has many treasures that come from the ground. Indians knew about these treasures and used them. They came to West Virginia to get salt. They found pools of oil. Some smeared the oil on their skins to keep insects away. Some drank the oil as medicine.

In 1607 England formed its first permanent settlement in America. This was in Jamestown, Virginia. The king of England made Virginia into a royal colony. This meant it was ruled by England.

For a long time what is now West Virginia was part of Virginia. It was called *western Virginia*.

In about 1669 John Lederer explored near where Harpers Ferry is today. He and his men are thought to be the first explorers in what is now West Virginia. A man named Morgan Morgan was probably the first non-Indian to build a home here. He came from the Delaware colony. With his long gun on his shoulder, Morgan Morgan walked into western Virginia. In about 1731 he built a log cabin near Bunker Hill. He brought his family there. They farmed the land. This one family did not disturb the Indians' hunting grounds.

In the 1730s, German people from Pennsylvania (pen • sill • VAY • nya) arrived. They built little towns near the rivers. The first was New Mecklenburg (MECK • lin • berg), now Shepherdstown (SHEP • erdz • town). People from parts of Europe came to western Virginia. They came from England, Scotland, Ireland, and Germany.

Shepherdstown, one of the early settlements in West Virginia

The settlers took the Indians' hunting grounds. There were bloody battles as the Indians fought to keep their lands. George Washington fought in battles against Indians in western Virginia.

The Indians made western Virginia dangerous. In 1763 the king of England ordered settlers to keep out. He said western Virginia was Indian land. The settlers didn't listen. Soon even more came. Some put their belongings on flatboats and traveled there on rivers.

To claim land, settlers made notches in trees with their axes. They called this "tomahawk rights." The

settlers then cut down trees and built log cabins. The
people grew corn. They hunted deer and elk. The cabin
fireplace was used to cook food. It also kept the people
warm. The settlers learned to make what they needed.
They made soap out of animal fat. Candles were made
out of beeswax or animal fat. Corn husks made good
brooms. People traded with each other. A family with
cows might trade milk for handwoven clothes.

Where many people settled in an area, towns grew.
Wheeling and Clarksburg began growing in the 1770s.

The Indians tried one last time to keep their lands. The Shawnee chief Cornstalk led a fight against the settlers. Chief Logan—whose family had been murdered by white settlers—joined in the fight. But there were too many soldiers against them. The Indians lost at Point Pleasant in 1774. They were driven out of western Virginia. Today, only about 800 Indians live in the state.

With Indian attacks ending, more settlers arrived. By 1775, about 30,000 settlers lived in western Virginia.

People in America had settled the land themselves. They had fought the Indians themselves. They disliked paying high taxes in England. They wanted to rule themselves.

In 1776 Americans formed a new country. It was called the United States of America. Americans had to fight the Revolutionary War to free themselves from England. People in western Virginia joined the fight for freedom. In 1782 the last battle of the Revolutionary War was fought at Wheeling. The Americans won the Revolutionary War.

Virginia became the 10th state in 1788. Western Virginia was still part of Virginia.

Eastern and western Virginia were like two different worlds. In the east, rich people owned big farms, called *plantations*. Tobacco was grown there. Black slaves did the work on these plantations.

In western Virginia most people had small farms. There were few slaves.

The people in western Virginia had many complaints. They felt that Virginia made them pay too much tax. They wanted more lawmakers. They said that they didn't have good schools or roads. For these reasons, western Virginians began to think about forming their own state in the early 1800s. It took them many years to get their wish.

Meanwhile, the people of western Virginia began to do more than farm and hunt. In 1797 salt drilling began in western Virginia. In 1815 natural gas was found by accident near Charleston. This became the first natural gas well in the U.S. Iron and steel mills were built throughout the 1800s. Coal mining became important. By 1855, many steamships and trains in America ran on western Virginia coal. Oil was discovered at Burning Springs. Nearby Parkersburg grew as a town where oil workers got supplies.

Pittsburgh Steel in Wheeling

Harpers Ferry, where the Shenandoah and Potomac rivers meet

In the late 1850s, Americans argued about slavery. Slave-owning Southerners—including Virginians— feared that the U. S. government would end slavery. Many Southerners said that each state should decide for itself about slavery and other issues. There was talk of war between Northern and Southern states.

In 1859 a man who hated slavery came to what is now West Virginia. His name was John Brown. His plan was to capture the United States arsenal at Harpers Ferry. Guns were kept there. Brown then planned to free slaves in Maryland and present-day Virginia.

Harpers Ferry National Historical Park

On October 16, 1859, John Brown and about 20 other men walked from a farm to the town of Harpers Ferry. They captured the arsenal. But U. S. Marines were sent in. There was a fierce gun battle at dawn. Two of John Brown's sons—and eight of his other men—were killed. John Brown was captured.

"Why did you do this?" he was asked. "I came to free the slaves!" he said. John Brown was given a trial, then hanged at Charles Town.

To people who disliked slavery, John Brown became a hero. Others called him a crazed troublemaker. The argument over slavery became more heated. Then the talking ended. The Civil War (1861-1865) began. On one side were the Northern, or Union (YOON • yun), states. On the other were the Southern, or Confederate (kahn • FED • er • ut), states.

Virginia was a Southern state. Many people owned slaves. Virginia lawmakers decided to secede from (leave) the United States. Virginia did this on April 17, 1861. Virginia soldiers joined the Confederate army.

Confederate States

Border States in the Union

Union States and Territories

You will remember that in the western part of Virginia there were few slaves. Most of the people there wanted to remain with the Union. They were allowed to form their own state. It was called West Virginia. West Virginia became the 35th state on June 20, 1863.

West Virginians didn't get to enjoy statehood. The Civil War was raging. West Virginia sent about 36,000 men to fight in the Union army. West Virginians often found themselves fighting friends and relatives.

The first railroad entered Harpers Ferry in 1863.

The first land battle of the Civil War was in West Virginia, at Philippi (fah • LIP • ee). There, Union soldiers beat Confederate troops. At one time Confederate troops under General "Stonewall" Jackson seized Harpers Ferry. But the Union got it back.

In 1863 Union soldiers won one of West Virginia's biggest battles. This was at Droop Mountain. As the Civil War continued the Union had more soldiers. It had better supplies. By 1865 the Union had won the Civil War.

After the Civil War, many railroads were built in West Virginia. Oil, lumber, and coal went by train to many cities in America.

Coal mines can be found throughout West Virginia.

West Virginia became a leading coal-mining state. West Virginia has soft—bituminous (by • TOOM • ih • nuss) —coal. It was needed to heat buildings, make steel, and run machines.

Miners went down into the ground to get the coal. During the 1800s they used picks to chop the coal from the face of the mine. Then the coal was shoveled into coal cars. Coal mining was back-breaking work. It was dangerous. Cave-ins sometimes buried miners. Deadly fumes smothered them. There were explosions, too. On December 6, 1907 there were huge explosions and fires in coal mines at Monongah (meh • NON • gah), killing 361. This is the biggest coal-mine disaster in U.S. history.

In the 1900s machines helped coal miners. Cutting machines removed the coal from the mines. Loading machines put it into the coal cars.

But the life of a miner was still very hard. Some got what we now call *black lung* disease. This comes from breathing coal dust underground. Miners still worked long hours—often 10 hours a day—for little pay. When the coal was "mined out" many lost their jobs. For these reasons, miners joined a *union*. It was called the United Mine Workers of America. They worked together for more pay and better working conditions.

Sometimes there was fighting between union miners and mine owners. In 1912 miners and mine guards fought with guns at Paint Creek and Cabin Creek mines. As many as 50 miners and guards may have died in these battles. In 1921 machine guns and airplanes were sent in

A glowing furnace at Seneca Glass Company

to fight the miners of Logan County. Slowly, miners got more pay. In 1968, 78 miners died in an explosion at Farmington. After that, the United States passed important laws to make mining safer.

Today, West Virginia is the second leading coal state. West Virginia has much more than coal. It is a big glassmaking state. Many people come to West Virginia to enjoy the mountains and warm spring waters.

You have learned about some of West Virginia's history. Now it is time for a trip—in words and pictures—through the Mountain State.

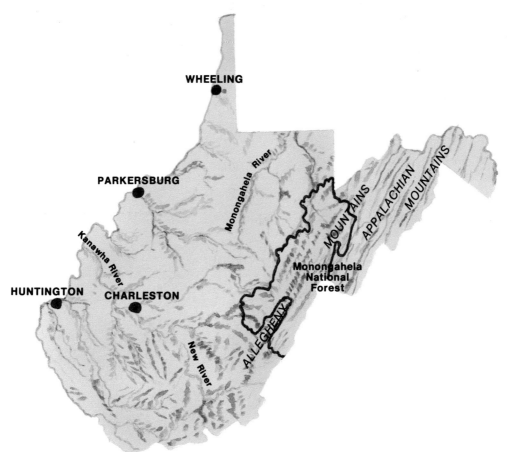

On a map, you can see that West Virginia has an odd

shape. It is shaped much like an apron. The apron string

on the left is called the *Northern Panhandle.* The apron

string on the right is called the *Eastern Panhandle.* Five

states border on West Virginia. They are Pennsylvania,

Maryland, Virginia, Kentucky, and Ohio.

You are in an airplane high above West Virginia. The

Allegheny (al • ah • GAY • nee) Mountains, part of the

Appalachians, reach up to your airplane. Rivers flow

through the mountains like blue threads.

Charleston, the capital of West Virginia

Your airplane is coming down through the mountains. You are landing in Charleston. To build the airport, the tops of mountains were chopped off! Then valleys were filled in with dirt to make a place where jets could land.

Long ago, Shawnee Indians hunted in this area. In the 1770s white settlers arrived. A few people came to the area to get salt. A famous explorer, Daniel Boone, built a log cabin for his family where Charleston now stands.

Charleston lies where two rivers—the Elk and the Kanawha (keh • NAW • wah)—flow together. In the 1800s people traveled to Charleston by wagon. From Charleston, they went by boat to other places. Some stayed there and built houses and stores.

23

Left: The State Capitol building is on the Kanawha River.
Right: The Cultural Center

Charleston has been West Virginia's capital since 1885. You can see the dome of the State Capitol building for miles around. The dome is the biggest of all 50 state capitols. Lawmakers from across West Virginia meet in the State Capitol building. You can watch them make laws for the Mountain State.

Just next to the State Capitol building, visit the Cultural Center. The State Museum is downstairs. There, you can learn about West Virginia history. You can learn how settlers came there and how they lived.

Sunrise

Visit "Sunrise," once the home of a West Virginia governor. Today, the big houses at "Sunrise" are museums. One is called the Charleston Art Gallery. There you can see famous paintings. At the Planetarium (plan • eh • TEAR • e • um) you can learn about the stars. At the Children's Museum you can learn about Indians.

Charleston is a big chemical-making city. Coal is mined in the area. Natural gas is found nearby. There are oil wells. Coal, gas, and oil are sent to Charleston factories. They are used to make chemicals.

Going northeast from Charleston you'll see coal mines. You'll see oil and gas wells pumping away. You'll see lovely towns in the valleys.

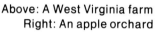
Above: A West Virginia farm
Right: An apple orchard

You'll also pass farms. West Virginia isn't a big
farming state. But farmers do raise beef cattle and
broiler chickens. Milk is another main farm product.
Corn is a main crop. Apples, grapes, pears, and plums are
grown in the state.

About 160 miles north of Charleston you'll come to the
city of Fairmont. Fairmont is in the northern part of the
state. It is in the heart of a big coal-mining area.

Visit Pricketts (PRICK • etts) Fort near Fairmont. In
1774 settlers here built a fort to protect themselves from
Indians. Over 200 years later the fort was rebuilt to
remind people of earlier times.

Pricketts Fort recreates living in the 18th century.
It was rebuilt in 1976.

Also, visit the house of Francis H. Pierpont (PEER •
pont) in Fairmont. He was a West Virginia lawmaker
when West Virginia was breaking away from Virginia.
Some call Pierpont the "Father of West Virginia."

One West Virginia father had a son who founded a
town. You remember Morgan Morgan, probably the first
settler in West Virginia. His son, Zackquill (ZAK • kwill)
Morgan, founded Morgantown in about 1766.

Morgantown is only about 15 miles northeast of
Fairmont. The city lies on the Monongahela (meh • NON •
gah • HE • lah) River. There are over 20 coal mines near
Morgantown. Two of the biggest coal mines in the world
are near there. Glassmaking is another big business.

Above: West Virginia University at Morgantown
Right: Wheeling Machine Products makes pipe fittings.

Morgantown is the home of West Virginia University. Students there study art, farming, medicine, and just about every other subject.

Visit the Core Arboretum (KOR ar • bor • EE • tum) at Morgantown. There you can see over 500 kinds of trees and plants that live in West Virginia.

Wheeling, on the Ohio River, is about 75 miles northwest of Morgantown. It is on the strip of land known as the Northern Panhandle, between Ohio and Pennsylvania.

Indians and settlers fought in the Wheeling area. Fort Henry was built to protect the settlers. This grew into the city of Wheeling.

"Mountaineers Are Always Free!" is West Virginia's state motto. Wheeling has played a big role in many fights for freedom. The last battle of the Revolutionary War was fought here. Later, Wheeling people helped slaves escape northward on the Underground Railroad.

Today, Wheeling is West Virginia's third biggest city. Metals, plastics, and glass are produced in Wheeling.

The Mansion Museum and Gallery is in beautiful Oglebay (oh • GEL • bay) Park. There you can learn about history and art.

Berkeley Springs is about 175 miles southeast of Wheeling. It is between Maryland and Virginia in the Eastern Panhandle. People bathe in the springs there.

Left: Berkeley Springs, a health resort in Morgan County
Below: The Mansion Museum and Gallery in Oglebay Park

A *spring* is water that bubbles out of the ground. It starts as rainwater that seeps into the ground. The water is heated by hot rocks underground. Then it comes out of the ground through cracks.

Today, the spring waters are piped into bathhouses. Minerals in the spring waters are thought to cure some diseases. White Sulphur Springs is another area where people bathe in the warm spring waters.

One of the most historic places in the United States is about 35 miles southeast of Berkeley Springs. This is Harpers Ferry. It lies where the Shenandoah (shen • en • DOE • ah) and Potomac (peh • TOE • mick) rivers meet.

Harpers Ferry

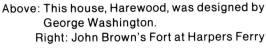
Above: This house, Harewood, was designed by
George Washington.
Right: John Brown's Fort at Harpers Ferry

You can see the "John Brown Fort," where he was beaten by Robert E. Lee and the U.S. Marines. Today Harpers Ferry is a National Historical Park. If he were alive today, John Brown would know many of the buildings at Harpers Ferry. They have been rebuilt to look as they did when he made his famous raid.

Visit Charles Town, just south of Harpers Ferry. Charles Town (a different place than Charleston) was named after Charles Washington. He was the younger brother of George Washington. Charles Washington founded Charles Town in 1786.

Left: The Jefferson County Courthouse
where John Brown was tried
Above: Seneca Rock

Visit the Jefferson County Courthouse in Charles
Town. This was where the John Brown trial was held.
While in jail, John Brown predicted that a Civil War
would occur.

Southwest of Charles Town is the Monongahela
National Forest. You'll see oak, spruce, pine, and maple
trees. Deer and bears still live there.

An unusual mountain is in Monongahela National
Forest. It is called Seneca (SEN • ah • kah) Rock. Seneca
Rock towers 1,000 feet above a valley.

Seneca Caverns

Near Seneca Rock visit Seneca Caverns. These are caves. Millions of years ago water carved out the caves. Later, Seneca Indians are thought to have lived there. West Virginia has other beautiful caves, such as Lost World Cave and Organ Cave.

After exploring caves within the earth, go to a place where outer space is studied. The National Radio Astronomy Observatory (NAH • shun • al RAY • dee • o ah • STRON • ah • me ob • ZERV • ah • tor • ee) is southwest of Seneca Caverns. It is at the town of Green Bank. Radio telescopes are there.

Astronomers use these radio telescopes. They study radio waves from stars. They learn about the stars from the radio waves. The radio telescopes have been used to "listen" for life on far-off worlds, too.

West Virginia mountains

Just west of the Green Bank radio telescopes you can visit the Cass Scenic Railroad. It will take you on a train ride through beautiful mountains.

Mountains made it hard to build roads and railroads through West Virginia. Mountains had to be blasted away. Bridges had to be built across mountain passes.

Tall stories were made up about one railroad builder. He was a black man named John Henry. According to the stories, John Henry weighed 44 pounds when he was born. Not only that, he was born with a hammer in his hand! John Henry became the best railroad builder of all. He swung a ten-pound hammer. He drove spikes into mountainsides. His job was to make a big hole. Then other men stuck dynamite inside. This way, the mountain was blasted away little by little.

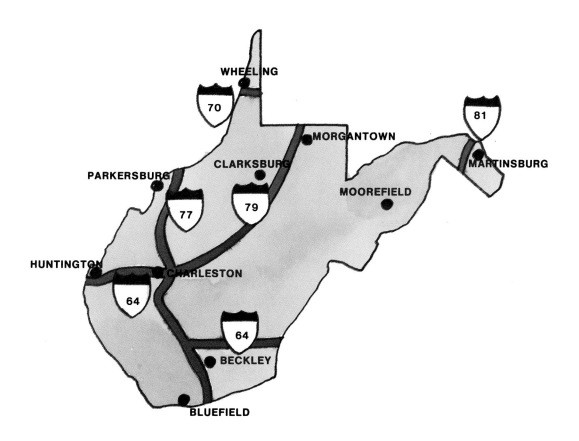

There was a new invention, however. It was a steam drill. People said it could drive through mountains better than a man. "No machine is better than a man!" said John Henry. He had a contest with the machine. People came to see who could make a bigger tunnel in the mountain. This was said to have occurred in West Virginia, at the Big Bend Tunnel. All day and all night John Henry hammered through the mountain. He beat the machine. But he had worked so hard he died—with a hammer in his hand.

To many people, West Virginia is best known for its coal. Would you like to see what a coal mine looks like? At Beckley, you can. You can learn about coal there.

To finish your trip, head about 100 miles northwest of Beckley to Huntington. Huntington is just about tied with Charleston as West Virginia's biggest city. Huntington lies in the far western part of the state, where the Ohio and Guyandotte (GUY • en • dot) rivers meet.

Huntington was founded in 1871. It was a stopping point for the Chesapeake (CHESS • ah • peek) and Ohio Railroad.

Below: The Ohio River
Right: Making glass at Blenko Glass Company

Left: A glassblower is both an artist and
a craftsman.
Above: Heritage Village

Today, Chemicals and metals are made in Huntington.
Glass and furniture are two other products. These go by
train or boat to many other cities.

Visit Heritage Village in Huntington. It shows what
this railroad city looked like 100 years ago. There, you
can see trains from long-ago days. You can also see the
old Bank of Huntington. It's quiet now. But on
September 8, 1875 it wasn't so quiet. A gang—thought
to be the Jesse James gang—robbed the bank.

Places can't tell the whole story of West Virginia.
Many interesting people have lived in the Mountain
State.

Thomas Jonathan Jackson was born in Clarksburg. He worked hard to become a teacher and a soldier. West Virginia was on the Northern side in the Civil War. But Jackson felt that he was still a Virginian, not a West Virginian. With other Virginians, he fought on the side of the South. Thomas Jackson became a great general. In one battle, his men were greatly outnumbered. But Jackson wouldn't let them back away from the fight. "There is Jackson standing like a stone wall," said another Southern general. "Stonewall" Jackson was one of the best Confederate generals.

When people argue, it is sometimes said that "They're just like the Hatfields and the McCoys." The Hatfields were a West Virginia family from Mingo and Logan counties. The McCoy family lived across the border in Kentucky. During the Civil War, they became enemies. Some think the fight started over a hog. For about 15 years, they had a famous family feud. The Hatfields and McCoys shot and often killed each other.

Left: An outdoor play about the Hatfields and the McCoys at Grandview State Park
Above: Pearl S. Buck's home

Jack Dempsey (DEM • see) was another fighter who lived in Logan County. Dempsey was born in Manassa (mah • NASS • ah), Colorado. But as a young man he came to West Virginia to work in the coal mines. He shoveled coal for 50¢ a carload. It helped make him tough. Jack Dempsey became one of the most famous of all heavyweight boxing champions. He was champion of the world from 1919-1926.

Pearl S. Buck was born in the town of Hillsboro, West Virginia. When she was very young, her family went to live in China. Pearl Buck could speak Chinese before she knew English. She became a great writer. She wrote about life in China. *The Good Earth* and *Dragon Seed* are two of her books.

West Virginia University

Booker T. Washington was born a slave in Virginia. But he moved to West Virginia. He worked hard and became a teacher. He founded a college for black people—Tuskegee Institute (tus • KEE • gee IN • sta • toot). Booker T. Washington became a great black leader. He told the story of his life in his book, *Up From Slavery.*

Walter Reuther (ROO • thur) was born in Wheeling. When he was 15, he became a steel worker. Later he became a union leader. Walter Reuther worked to improve the lives of people who make cars.

Jerry West was born in the town of Cabin Creek. He played basketball at West Virginia University. Later he played pro basketball in the NBA. Jerry West scored over 25,000 points in his pro career. In one game alone he scored 63. He is one of the all-time greats of basketball.

Mother's Day Church
in Grafton

There is a day in May when people honor their
mothers. Anna Jarvis, born in Grafton, West Virginia,
founded this special day. It is called Mother's Day.

Home to Mound Builders . . . Shawnee Indians . . .
"Stonewall" Jackson . . . and Anna Jarvis.

A beautiful state of mountains . . . caves . . . rivers
. . . and warm springs.

A leading state for coal mining and glassmaking.

The scene of John Brown's famous raid.

A place where farmers talk of "falling out of" their
fields . . . and where astronomers listen to signals from
space.

This is West Virginia—the Mountain State.

Facts About WEST VIRGINIA

Area—24,181 square miles (41st biggest state)

Greatest Distance North to South—237 miles

Greatest Distance East to West—265 miles

Border States—Pennsylvania, Maryland, Virginia, Kentucky, Ohio

Highest Point—4,862 feet above sea level (Spruce Knob)

Lowest Point—240 Feet above sea level (on the shores of the Potomac River)

Hottest Recorded Temperature—112° (at Moorefield on August 4, 1930; also at Martinsburg on July 10, 1936)

Coldest Recorded Temperature—Minus 37° (at Lewisburg on December 30, 1917)

Statehood—Our 35th state, on June 20, 1863

Origin of Name West Virginia—Virginia was named after Elizabeth, the "Virgin Queen" of England; when the western part of Virginia became a state, it was called West Virginia

Capital—Charleston (1885)

Previous Capitals—Wheeling from 1863-1870; then Charleston from 1870-1875; then Wheeling again from 1875-1885

Counties—55

U.S. Senators—2

U.S. Representatives—4

Electoral Votes—6

State Senators—34

State Delegates—100

State Songs—"The West Virginia Hills"; "West Virginia, My Home Sweet Home"; and "This is My West Virginia"

State Motto—*Montani Semper Liberi* (Latin meaning "Mountaineers Are Always Free")

Nicknames—The Mountain State, The Coal Bin of the World, Almost Heaven

State Seal—Adopted the year of statehood, in 1863

State Flag—Adopted in 1929

State Flower—Rhododendron

State Bird—Cardinal

State Animal—Black bear

State Tree—Sugar maple

State colors—Blue and gold (unofficial)

Some Colleges and Universities—Bethany College, Marshall University, West Liberty State College, West Virginia State College, West Virginia University, Wheeling College

Some Rivers—Ohio, Kanawha, Monongahela, Big Sandy, Guyandotte, Little Kanawha, Elk

Chief Waterfall—Blackwater Falls

Some Caves—Seneca Caverns, Organ Cave, Smoke Hole Cavern, Lost World

National Forests—3 (Monongahela, George Washington, and Jefferson)

National Historical Parks—2 (Harpers Ferry and also the Chesapeake and Ohio Canal)

Animals—White-tailed deer, black bears, wildcats, foxes, raccoons, opossums, beavers, river otters, skunks, squirrels, rabbits, bats, wild turkeys, grouse, quail, owls, hawks, eagles, many other kinds of birds, rattlesnakes, copperheads, puff adders, turtles, frogs, lizards

Fishing—Bass, trout, pike

Farm Products—Milk, beef cattle, broiler chickens, corn, apples, peaches, pears, grapes, plums, blackberries, tobacco, potatoes, oats, wheat

Mining—Coal, natural gas, oil, limestone, sandstone, salt

Manufacturing Products—Chemicals, steel and other metals, glass products, pottery, tools and other metal products, food products

Population—1,949,644 (1980 census); 34th most populous state

Major Cities—Charleston   63,968   (all around 1980 census)
Huntington	63,684
Wheeling	43,070
Parkersburg	39,967
Morgantown	27,607
Weirton	24,736

West Virginia History

People lived in West Virginia at least 10,000 years ago; one early group was called the Mound Builders, who were really Adena Indians.

1607—The English form their first permanent colony in America at Jamestown, Virginia

1624—Virginia becomes a royal English colony; western Virginia is part of it

1669—John Lederer, a German doctor, explores western Virginia about this time

1727—New Mecklenberg (now Shepherdstown) built by Pennsylvania Germans about now

1731—Morgan Morgan, probably the first settler in West Virginia, builds a log cabin at Bunker Hill about this time

1742—Coal discovered on Coal River

1748—George Washington surveys western Virginia for English Lord Fairfax

1754—George Washington fights French and Indians in western Virginia during French and Indian War

1763—English have stronger control of area after winning French and Indian War

1774—Indians are beaten at Point Pleasant and forced to give up their claims to the area

1776—Western Virginians begin trying to separate themselves from Virginia

1783—United States has been born as Americans win Revolutionary War

1788—Virginia becomes a state with western Virginia part of it

1788—Charleston founded as Fort Lee

1800—Population of western Virginia is 78,592; most people want it to become a separate state

1815—Natural gas is discovered near Charleston; this becomes the first natural gas well in the U.S.

1818—National Road—used by settlers in covered wagons—reaches Wheeling

1836—First railroad in state at Harpers Ferry

1859—John Brown raids arsenal at Harpers Ferry

1860—Western Virginia's first oil well is drilled at Burning Springs; nearby Parkersburg grows as a place to get supplies

1861—Start of Civil War; Virginia secedes from Union; western Virginians stay part of Union and work to form their own state

1863—On June 20, West Virginia becomes the 35th state

1863—Union wins Battle of Droop Mountain on November 6

1865—Civil War ends

1867—West Virginia University founded

1871—Huntington is founded

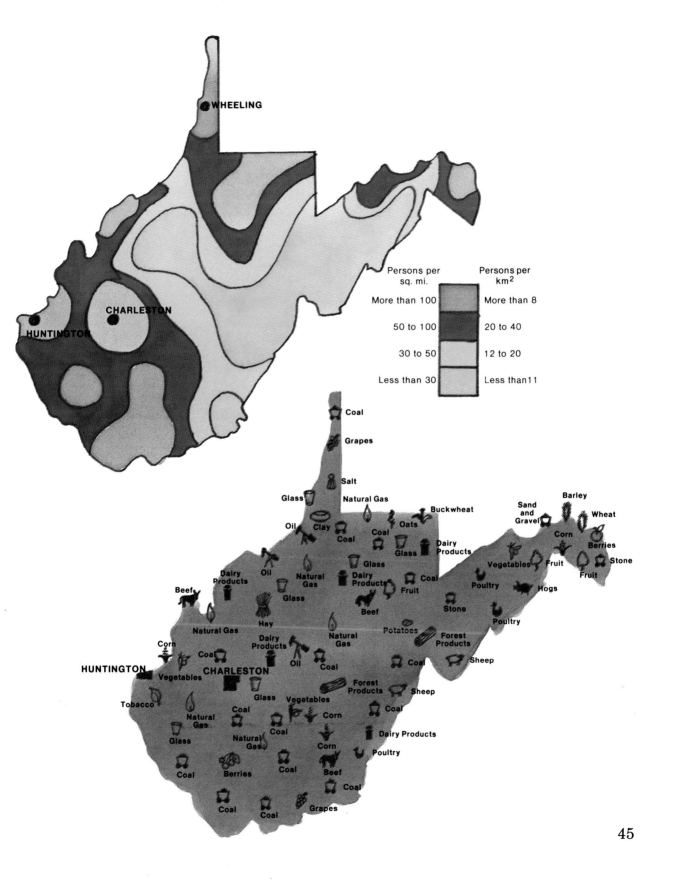

Persons per
sq. mi.

More than 100

50 to 100

30 to 50

Less than 30

Persons per
km²

More than 8

20 to 40

12 to 20

Less than 11

WHEELING

CHARLESTON

HUNTINGTON

Coal

Grapes

Salt

Glass

Natural Gas

Buckwheat

Sand and Gravel

Barley

Wheat

Oil

Clay

Coal

Coal

Oats

Corn

Berries

Stone

Glass

Dairy Products

Vegetables

Fruit

Fruit

Oil

Dairy Products

Natural Gas

Glass

Dairy Products

Coal

Fruit

Poultry

Hogs

Beef

Dairy Products

Glass

Beef

Stone

Poultry

Natural Gas

Hay

Natural Gas

Potatoes

Forest Products

Corn

Dairy Products

Natural Gas

HUNTINGTON

Coal

CHARLESTON

Oil

Coal

Coal

Sheep

Vegetables

Forest Products

Sheep

Tobacco

Glass

Vegetables

Coal

Natural Gas

Coal

Corn

Dairy Products

Glass

Natural Gas

Corn

Poultry

Coal

Berries

Coal

Beef

Coal

Coal

Coal

Grapes

45

1872—Present state constitution is adopted

1885—Charleston becomes the state capital

1900—Population of West Virginia is 950,800

1907—In this one year, 537 are killed in five mine explosions

1912 and 1913—Miners, trying to improve working conditions, battle mine guards at Paint Creek and Cabin Creek mines

1914-1918—During World War I, 45,648 West Virginians serve

1920-1921—Coal miners fight with mine guards and police in Mingo and Logan counties

1932—State Capitol building at Charleston is completed

1940—92 miners die in explosion at Bartley

1939-1945—During World War II, West Virginia supplies coal, steel, and chemicals for the war effort

1954—West Virginia Turnpike is completed

1959—National Radio Astronomy Observatory opens at Green Bank

1968—78 coal miners are trapped and killed at Farmington

1970—Law is signed to protect the health and safety of the nation's coal miners

1972—Huge flood kills over 100 people on Buffalo Creek in Logan County

1977—Senator Robert C. Byrd of West Virginia becomes U.S. Senate Majority Leader

INDEX

About the Author:

Dennis Fradin attended Northwestern University on a creative writing scholarship and graduated in 1967. While still at Northwestern, he published his first stories in *Ingenue* magazine and also won a prize in *Seventeen's* short story competition. A prolific writer, Dennis Fradin has been regularly publishing stories in such diverse places as *The Saturday Evening Post, Scholastic, National Humane Review, Midwest,* and *The Teaching Paper.* He has also scripted several educational films. Since 1970 he has taught second grade reading in a Chicago school—a rewarding job, which, the author says, "provides a captive audience on whom I test my children's stories." Married and the father of three children, Dennis Fradin spends his free time with his family or playing a myriad of sports and games with his childhood chums.

About the Artists:

Len Meents studied painting and drawing at Southern Illinois University and after graduation in 1969 he moved to Chicago. Mr. Meents works full time as a painter and illustrator. He and his wife and child currently make their home in LaGrange, Illinois.

Richard Wahl, graduate of the Art Center College of Design in Los Angeles, has illustrated a number of magazine articles and booklets. He is a skilled artist and photographer who advocates realistic interpretations of his subjects. He lives with his wife and two sons in Libertyville, Illinois.

DATE DUE

NOV 19 '85 JD	MAR 4/N		
JAN 28 '86 NK			
FEB 18 '86 SS			
KG			
FEB 5 '87 NK			
MAY 13 '87 JD			
SEP 24 '87 GK			
MAY 1 2 C			
APR 28 '89 TV			
TV			
MAR 20 KM			
1-6-94 CT			
NOV 1 NK			
NOV 8 NK			
NOV 1 CG			
NOV 1 4 K			
CB			

HIGHSMITH 45-220